SUCCESS

All rights reserved. Copyright
2024 by Madiop Auguste DIALLO
ISBN no.: 9798320790237

Legal deposit: March 2024

Foreword

The book "SUCCEED" **is** an inspiring work dedicated to all those who aspire to improve their financial situation by creating passive income, even from limited initial capital. This practical guide is the fruit of years of research and experience in the field of investment and entrepreneurship.

"Succeed" stands out for its down-to-earth, accessible approach, making personal finance understandable to the average reader who might feel intimidated by the complex jargon often associated with the world of investment and entrepreneurship.

With a balanced combination of strategic advice, case studies, and practical exercises, this book is both a primer and an action plan for anyone looking to build a more stable and prosperous financial future.

Through its pages, I share not only my knowledge, but also my philosophy that financial success is possible for everyone. I emphasize the importance of patience, ongoing education and perseverance. In addition, "Succeed" highlights the impact of community and family support in the journey to success, recognizing that behind every success story are mentors, friends and loved ones who have offered help and encouragement.

Intended for beginners as well as those already initiated into the principles of creating passive income, "Succeed" is more than a book: it's a source of inspiration, a call to action for those who dream of financial freedom but don't know where to start. In a world where economic uncertainty can seem daunting, "Succeed" offers hope, direction and the promise that, with the right strategies and a supportive network, financial success is well within reach.

Introduction

SUCCESS is a broad, personal concept that encompasses much more than simply achieving specific goals. It's a process that combines self-discovery, perseverance and continuous adaptation to life's challenges. This theme, explored through the ages in literature, philosophy, and psychology, continues to arouse deep interest for its potential to transform our personal, professional, and spiritual lives.

At the heart of success is the idea of personal growth and fulfillment. It's not just about reaching a specific peak, but rather about traveling a path that is itself enriching and meaningful. Success encompasses the ability to set ambitious but achievable goals, to face adversity with resilience, to learn from failure, and above all, to remain true to one's values and convictions throughout this quest.

In a society often focused on tangible, material success, it's important to remember that success is also inner and deeply personal. It is measured by the happiness, satisfaction and sense of fulfillment that comes from pursuing one's passions and making a positive contribution to the community.

This rich and complex concept will be explored in the following pages, not only through theories and philosophical reflections, but also through inspiring stories of people who have been able to define and achieve their own version of success. The aim is to provide readers with the tools, ideas and inspiration to pursue their own quest for success, whatever path they choose.

Success, a term so commonly used, but whose essence sometimes seems elusive, is here broken down into chapters that plumb the depths of our ambitions, motivations and aspirations. This journey to the heart of success is not limited to the conquest of professional heights or the accumulation of material goods. It also questions the fullness of existence, the quality of our relationships, the pursuit of our passions, and our ability to contribute to a better world.

At the dawn of a new millennium, when the world seems to be spinning at breakneck speed and the traditional definitions of success and achievement are constantly being called into question, it has never been more crucial to examine what it really means to "succeed". This book, designed as a compass for the soul as well as the mind, explores the many facets of success, through prisms often overlooked by mainstream discourse.

This book invites you to introspect, to question your own criteria for success in a healthy way, and to explore ways of achieving lasting, authentic satisfaction in your lives.

We offer reflections nourished by the human sciences, inspiring testimonials from personalities who have achieved remarkable forms of success, and practical exercises designed to help you chart your own path to success. These tools are there to guide you, but it's your personal commitment, your will to surpass yourself, that will be the real driving force behind your success.

In short, this book is not just for reading, but for living. It is a companion in your personal quest for success.

Chapter 1. The Definition of Success

According to Romy SCHNEIDR, "*Success isn't always what it seems.*

It's not about becoming famous,

Neither rich nor powerful.

To be successful is to get out of bed in the morning and be happy.

what we're going to do during the day,

So happy it feels like flying.

It means working with people you love.

Success means being in touch with the world and communicating your passion.

It's going to bed at night thinking

we did the best we could.

To succeed is to experience joy,

freedom, friendship and love.

I would say that to succeed is to Love."

This quote encapsulates a profound and emotionally rich vision of success. It moves away from the conventional parameters of wealth, power or fame, to embrace a more intimate definition of success centered around personal well-being and fulfillment.

Everyday Joy

The notion that "success is getting out of bed in the morning and being happy about what you're going to do during the day" highlights the importance of finding pleasure and satisfaction in daily activities. This underlines the value of a passion for one's work, which is measured not in terms of external success, but in the sense of personal fulfillment it brings.

Human Relations

The emphasis on relationships - "working with people you love" - resonates with the idea that success is lived and shared with others. Enriching human interactions are often the greatest rewards for our efforts, emphasizing that professional success is only truly complete when accompanied by relational and social success.

Communication and Sharing

The commitment to "being in touch with the world and communicating our passion" speaks to the importance of opening up to others and sharing what motivates us. This implies a vulnerability and authenticity that isn't always easy, but is essential for an authentic sense of achievement and belonging.

Reflection and Inner Satisfaction

The idea of "going to bed at night telling yourself you did the best you could" evokes a form of personal reflection where success is intrinsically linked to personal effort and growth. It's a recognition that perfection is not the goal; true success is about striving, learning and evolving.

Love and Connection

Finally, concluding that "to succeed is to love" is a powerful affirmation of love as the ultimate measure of success. This goes beyond romantic love to encompass self-love, friendship, and an empathetic connection with community and environment. Love is seen not just as an emotion, but as a daily action that enriches our experience of life.

However, the essence of this quote beautifully captures a holistic and deeply human perspective on success. It suggests that true success transcends visible, material achievements to touch on the quality of our life experience, our relationships, and our ability to love and be passionate about what we do. Regardless of its author, the message remains powerful and inspiring, encouraging a personal re-evaluation of what it really means to "succeed" in life.

This reflection on success reminds us that the most significant measures of success are often intangible. They lie not in what we have or who we are in the eyes of others, but rather in the quality of our lived experience, the depth of our relationships, and the authenticity of our engagement with the world around us.

Success is a vast, multi-faceted concept that goes far beyond the simple acquisition of wealth or professional recognition. It touches on different dimensions of human life, encompassing personal and professional success, and sometimes even the meaning we give to our contribution to the world. To explore success is to plunge into a quest for fulfillment that is both unique to each individual and universal in its aspiration.

Here are some dimensions through which success can be perceived:

1. **Personal Success** On a personal level, success can mean achieving much-desired life goals, such as fulfilling a long-held dream, achieving work-life balance, or cultivating a sense of satisfaction and

happiness. It also includes personal development, such as self-improvement, the acquisition of new skills, or emotional and intellectual growth.

2. **Professional Success**

In the professional or business context, success is often measured by achievements such as career advancement, innovation, significant contribution to a specific field, or the creation of a successful business. It can also be measured in financial terms, such as revenue, profitability, or market share.

3. **Social Impact**

For some, success takes on a more collective or altruistic dimension. This refers to the impact a person or organization has on their community, country, or even on a global scale, such as contributing to social, environmental or educational progress, positively influencing the lives of others, or working for social justice.

4. **Recognition and Esteem**

Another aspect of success can be recognition by one's peers, whether through awards, distinctions, or simply the respect and admiration of those around one. For some, success is intimately linked to the sense of personal accomplishment that comes from this recognition.

5. **Balance and Harmony**

Increasingly, success is also seen in terms of the ability to achieve a healthy balance between different aspects of life, such as work, family, leisure and personal well-being. For many, success means being able to reconcile these various elements in a balanced and harmonious way.

6. **Impact and Contribution**

The noblest aspect of success might be the impact you have on the world and the people around you. This can take the form of significant contributions to society, such as supporting the underprivileged, advancing important causes, or helping to solve global problems. Success, in this context, is measured not in terms of what one acquires, but of what one gives. In short, success is a multidimensional, deeply personal and evolving concept. What constitutes success for one person may be radically different for another, reflecting the diversity of human values, goals and aspirations.

Success as Process

Perhaps the most crucial aspect of success is to conceive of it not as an end point, but as a process. It is dynamic, evolving with our dreams, goals and values. Success is also marked by the ability to adapt, to overcome failure, and to pursue personal growth. It is intrinsic to the quest for meaning and purpose in life, involving constant introspection and re-evaluation of goals and aspirations.

Chapter 2. Self-knowledge

Believing in yourself is essential when you aspire to succeed. This inner belief acts not only as a motivating force, but also as a shield against the doubts and obstacles that arise on the way to achieving our goals. Here are a few strategies for boosting self-confidence and forging a success-oriented mindset:

1. **Set Realistic Goals**

Start small. Set yourself realistic, achievable short-term goals. Achieving these small goals builds a solid foundation of self confidence, preparing you for bigger challenges.

2. **Celebrate every Victory**

No matter how big or small the achievement, take the time to celebrate it. It reinforces your belief in your abilities and motivates you for what's to come.

3. **Learn from Failure**

Treat every failure as a valuable lesson, not as proof of your inabilities. Failure is a natural step in the process of learning and personal growth.

4. **Positive entourage**

Surround yourself with people who support you, encourage you and believe in your abilities. Avoid toxic people who undermine your confidence and self-esteem.

5. **Personal Development**

Invest in your personal development through reading, training, workshops, etc. Improving your skills and acquiring new knowledge can significantly boost your confidence.

6. **Positive visualization**

Practice positive visualization. Imagine yourself reaching your goals and succeeding. This technique can boost self-confidence and motivation.

7. **Positive self-talk**

Pay attention to your self-talk. Replace negative, self-destructive thoughts with positive, constructive affirmations. How you talk to yourself can have a profound impact on your self-confidence.

8. **Take Calculated Risks**

Get out of your comfort zone and take calculated risks. Every new experience is an opportunity to prove that you can face the unknown and succeed.

9. **Exercise and Well-being**

Regular exercise improves not only physical health but also mental health, increasing feelings of well-being and self-confidence.

10. **Meditation and Mindfulness**

Meditation and the practice of mindfulness can help reduce stress and anxiety, promoting a calmer, more confident state of mind.

Ultimately, believing in yourself isn't a trait you have or don't have, but a quality you can develop with time and effort. By focusing on these strategies, you'll build a robust self-confidence that will serve as a solid foundation for achieving success in all aspects of your life.

Chapter 3: Setting achievable goals

Setting achievable goals is an essential process for personal and professional development. It not only helps to channel your energy towards specific goals, but also promotes motivation, focus and, ultimately, the achievement of those goals. Here are some key steps to setting achievable goals:

1. **Be Specific**

Well-defined goals are easier to achieve. Instead of saying "I want to be in better shape", opt for "I want to run 5 km in under 30 minutes within six months". Specificity clarifies the goal and makes it easier to measure progress.

2. **Make sure they're Measurable**

To know whether you've achieved your goal, you need to be able to measure it. Define clear criteria for progress and achievement. For example, "increase sales by 20% by the end of the year" is a measurable objective.

3. **Make them achievable**

It's important that your goals are realistic and achievable with the resources and time you have available. Setting goals that are too ambitious can lead to frustration. Consider your current limitations and plan rationally.

4. **Be Relevant**

Your goals must be meaningful to you and align with your values and long-term goals. If a goal doesn't excite you or contribute significantly to your longer-term vision, it may not be appropriate.

5. **Set Deadlines**

A goal without a deadline is often postponed indefinitely. Set a realistic deadline for achieving your goal. This creates a sense of urgency that can spur you into action.

6. **Focus them**

Large or long-term goals can seem daunting. To increase your chances of success, break them down into smaller, manageable sub-goals. This makes the process less overwhelming and offers regular opportunities to celebrate success along the way.

7. **Write them down**

Putting your goals in writing can increase your commitment to them. A tangible goals document or chart can serve as a constant reminder of what you're striving to achieve.

8. **Evaluate and Adjust**

The path to achieving a goal is not always linear. It's important to regularly assess your progress and be ready to adjust your plans if necessary. Flexibility can be crucial in overcoming unforeseen obstacles.

By following these steps, you can set goals that are not only achievable, but also inspiring and motivating. Remember that the key to success often lies in **perseverance**, **adaptability** and **careful planning**.

Chapter 4. Perseverance

Perseverance is an essential trait on the road to success. It can be defined as the unshakeable determination to pursue a goal or follow a path, despite the difficulties, obstacles and disappointments that may arise. This ability to persevere, even in the face of adversity, is often what separates those who achieve their goals from those who give up. Let's explore why perseverance is so crucial to success.

The Value of Perseverance

1. Overcoming Failures: Failures and setbacks are natural components of any growth or achievement process. Perseverance enables us to see these failures not as end points, but as stages, lessons to be learned in order to progress.

2. Time and Patience: Some ambitions, especially worthwhile ones, take time to realize. Perseverance instills the patience needed to wait for those results without getting discouraged.

3. Personal Growth: The road to success, paved with challenges and difficulties, offers countless opportunities for personal growth. Persevering through difficulties can increase resilience, self-confidence, and the ability to handle future challenges.

4. Passion and Motivation: Perseverance is often fueled by a deep passion for the goal at hand. This passion provides the motivation to keep going, even when circumstances seem insurmountable.

Cultivating Perseverance**Developing a Growth Mentality**: Believing in the ability to grow and improve through effort and learning can encourage perseverance. This mentality allows you to see challenges as opportunities to evolve.

Setting Achievable Goals: As mentioned above, breaking down a big goal into smaller, more manageable ones can help maintain motivation and perseverance.

Remembering the 'Why': Remembering why you're pursuing a goal can rekindle motivation in difficult times. This can involve thinking deeply about one's values and aspirations.

Seeking Support: Surrounding yourself with people who encourage and support your ambitions can provide the emotional safety net needed to persevere.

Learning from Mentors: Drawing inspiration from those who have succeeded before us can offer valuable lessons on how to navigate challenges and stay resolute.

Overcoming Obstacles**

1. Resilience in the face of Adversity**: Perseverance enables us to face obstacles, failures and setbacks that are inevitable on the road to

success. It encourages learning from difficulties rather than giving up in the face of them.

2. Managing Challenges:
The ability to persevere enables you to deal with challenges more constructively, by seeking solutions, finding alternatives, and staying focused on the end goals despite the obstacles encountered.

Achieving Goals

3. Discipline and Consistency:
Perseverance requires self-discipline and consistency in one's efforts to progress towards a goal. This promotes productivity and steady progress.

4. Determination and Motivation:
Perseverance nurtures the determination and motivation needed to keep going, even when the going gets tough. It's this inner strength that keeps the flame burning in moments of doubt and discouragement.

Achievement and Realization
5. Achieving Goals:Ultimately, perseverance is often the trait that turns dreams into reality. It's the will to keep going despite the obstacles that ultimately leads to the achievement of set goals.

6. Satisfaction and pride: Perseverance brings deep satisfaction and personal pride when goals are achieved after hard work and sustained commitment. This satisfaction often goes beyond mere material results to include a sense of personal accomplishment.

Perseverance is without doubt one of the most fundamental keys to success. It plays an essential role in the realization of goals and aspirations, in the management of challenges and setbacks, and in personal and professional development.

In conclusion, perseverance is not just a virtue in itself; it is a fundamental vector through which visions become reality. It involves committing oneself fully to the process, learning from every step backwards, and staying fixed on the goal, no matter what the obstacles. So, whatever your personal definition of success, perseverance will always be the beating heart that brings those ambitions to life.

Chapter 5: Surround yourself with the good guys

Surrounding yourself with the right people is an essential strategy for success and personal well-being. The people around you can have a profound influence on your life, your choices and your state of mind. Here are just a few reasons why it's important to surround yourself with the right people:

Positive influence

1. Encouragement and support: The right people will offer you unconditional support in your time of need, encouraging you to pursue your goals and believe in yourself. Their support can boost your motivation and self-confidence.

2. Inspiration and Role Models: Surrounding yourself with positive, successful people can inspire you to achieve your own goals. You can learn from their successes, mistakes and experiences to guide you on your own path to success.

Energy and Enthusiasm

3. Positive Energy:
Good people bring positive energy into your life. Their optimism, enthusiasm and constructive attitude can lift your own mood and help you face challenges with a positive outlook.

4. Personal Growth:
Good people encourage you to step out of your comfort zone, challenge your limits and push yourself to improve. They can help you develop new skills, gain different perspectives and broaden your worldview.

Healthy Environment

5. Negativity Avoidance:
Surrounding yourself with the right people often means keeping negative influences out of your life. Avoiding toxic people, constant criticism and harmful energies can help you maintain a healthy, positive mental attitude.

6. Creating a Strong Network:
By building meaningful relationships with quality people, you can create a strong network that can support your aspirations, open up professional and personal opportunities, and offer you valuable advice.

Emotional Well-Being

7. Sharing Joy and Sorrow:
The right people will be there to celebrate your successes with you, and support you in difficult times. Sharing experiences, feelings and precious moments can strengthen your relationships and enrich your life.

8. Strengthening Relationships:
Healthy, positive relationships can enhance your emotional well-being, reduce stress and foster a sense of connection and belonging. It can also encourage mutual support and genuine camaraderie.

Ultimately, then, surrounding yourself with the right people can stimulate your growth, enrich your emotional life, and strengthen your path to success. These can be mentors, close friends, family members or colleagues who share your values, aspirations and encourage you to become the best version of yourself.

Chapter 6. Time Management

Time management is a crucial element in leading a productive, balanced and fulfilled life. By managing your time effectively, you can optimize your efficiency, reduce stress and achieve your goals more efficiently. Here are some strategies to improve your time management:

1. Planning

- **Prioritize**: Identify your most important tasks and prioritize them according to urgency and importance.

- Create a Schedule**: Use a diary, to-do lists or planning tools to organize your days and weeks.

2. Goal Setting

- **SMART Goals**: Set specific, measurable, achievable, relevant and time-defined goals to guide you in using your time more strategically.

- **Divide Tasks**: Break down your goals into smaller, more manageable tasks to make the process more achievable and less daunting.

3. Eliminate Distractions

- **Email and Notification Management**: Limit your time spent on e-mails and social networks by setting specific times to check them.

- Creating a Supportive Environment**: Identify sources of distraction in your work environment and try to eliminate or minimize them.

4. Time Management Techniques

- **Pomodoro Technique**: Work in short time intervals followed by short breaks to maintain productivity and focus.

- **Eisenhower Matrix**: Rank your tasks according to urgency and importance to determine where to focus your time and energy.

5. Flexibility and Adaptability

 - **Regular Reassessment**: Review your progress, adjust your plan if necessary, and be ready to adapt your schedule to changing circumstances.

 - **Learn to Manage Mistakes**: Accept that mistakes or delays may occur, learn from these experiences and use them to improve in the future.

6. Delegate and Set Limits

 - **Delegate Tasks**: If possible, delegate certain tasks to others so that you can concentrate on the most important tasks requiring your expertise.

 - **Set Boundaries**: Learn to say no to commitments that don't contribute to your main objectives, and set clear limits to protect your time and energy.

By putting these time management strategies and techniques into practice, you can optimize your use of time, improve your productivity and find an effective balance between your professional and personal life. The aim is to turn your time into a valuable resource and use it in ways that bring you closer to your goals and personal fulfillment.

Chapter 7. Getting to know banks

The world of banking may seem complex at first glance, with its technical jargon and variety of products and services. Yet understanding the fundamentals of this sector is essential to managing personal and business finances effectively. This chapter aims to demystify banks, how they operate and their role in the economy.

1. Introduction to Banking

Banks are financial institutions that offer a range of services such as money deposit, credit, money transfers and financial advice, among others. They play a crucial role in the economy by acting as intermediaries between savers, who provide capital, and borrowers, who require funds.

2. How a bank works

The core of the banking business is based on the principle of financial intermediation.

Banks collect deposits from customers and use them to grant loans to other customers. The difference between the interest they pay on deposits and the interest they receive on loans is one of their main sources of income, known as the interest margin.

3. Banking Services

a. Deposit services

Deposit accounts enable customers to keep their money safe. This includes current accounts, used for day-to-day transactions, and savings accounts, which offer an interest rate in exchange for locking in funds.

b. Credits and loans

Banks offer various forms of credit, from personal loans to mortgages, meeting the varied financial needs of their customers. Credit conditions, such as interest rates and repayment terms, can vary considerably.

c. Payment services

Payment services, including credit and debit cards, bank transfers, and online payments, facilitate the movement of money in the economy and between individuals.

4. Bank regulation

The stability of the banking system is crucial to the economy. Banks are therefore subject to strict regulations designed to guarantee their solvency and protect deposits. Regulators require banks to maintain a minimum level of equity and comply with prudential standards.

5. Technological innovations and banking

The advent of digital technologies has profoundly transformed the banking sector. Online and mobile banking services now offer unprecedented convenience and accessibility, enabling users to carry out most of their financial transactions remotely. At the same time, the emergence of financial technologies (fintech) is pushing traditional banks to innovate in order to remain competitive.

**Case study **

Marc is a young professional who has just begun to navigate the world of personal finance. He's saved a substantial amount of money from his first job and now wants to invest it in a bank, but feels overwhelmed by the number of options available: current accounts, savings accounts, CDs (certificates of deposit), online accounts, etc. He wants to maximize his return while still having easy access to his funds in case of emergency. He wants to maximize his return while having easy access to his funds in case of emergency.

**Data **

- Initial amount to invest: €10,000

- Objective: Maximize return while maintaining access to funds

- Preferences: Marc prefers to have part of his money easily accessible and the other part in an option offering a better return over time.

**Exercise **

1. **Researching Accounts ** Mark must first research the different types of bank accounts:

   A. **Current Account ** Useful for daily transactions, with easy
access but little or no interest.
   B. **Savings Account ** Offers a higher interest rate than current accounts, ideal for storing emergency funds or saving for the short to medium term.
   C. **Certificate of Deposit (CD) ** Locks in your money for one year. fixed period (e.g. 1, 2, 5 years) with a generally higher interest rate, suitable for long-term savings

with no immediate need for access.

D. **Online Savings Accounts :** Often, these accounts offer higher interest rates than traditional banks and decent accessibility via digital platforms.

2. **Situation Analysis:** Marc should analyze his financial situation and risk tolerance to divide his money between accounts. Let's say he wants to keep €3,000 accessible for emergencies and invest the rest for long-term growth.

3. **Action Plan:**

   A. Place €3,000 in a **savings account** with a good interest rate and easy accessibility.
   B. With the remaining €7,000, Marc might consider splitting it between a **CD** and an **online savings account** to maximize returns while maintaining flexibility. For example, €3,500 in a CD with a 2-year term, and €3,500 in an online savings account offering a competitive interest rate.

4. **Interest calculation ** Marc should calculate the expected interest for each option based on annual interest rates. This will allow him to compare potential returns.

5. **Reassess ** Adjust the strategy every 6 to 12 months based on interest rate trends, personal needs and financial objectives.

**Conclusion of exercise : **

This exercise will help Mark understand the importance of choosing the right type of bank account based on his specific financial needs and objectives. By following these steps, he can maximize his return while maintaining the necessary access to his funds for emergencies or sudden opportunities.
**Case in point:

Emma is a busy Masters student who juggles her studies, a part-time job, and her passions such as yoga and painting. She often feels overwhelmed and has difficulty managing her time effectively, which causes her stress and prevents her from enjoying her leisure activities.

**Specific data : **

- University courses: 20 hours per week
- Part-time work: 15 hours per week

- Yoga: 3 hours per week

- Painting: 4 hours per week

- Self-study and homework: 15 hours per week

**Objective: ** Emma wants to optimize her schedule to balance her studies, work and hobbies, and give herself periods of rest.

**Exercise : **

1. **Activity inventory: ** Make a list of all Emma's activities and the time she wants to devote to them each week.

2. **Prioritization: ** Emma must prioritize her activities. Classes and work are her top

priorities, followed by her personal studies/duties, yoga, and finally painting as a relaxing activity.

3. **Time budget : ** Calculate total time available per week (168 hours), then subtract non-negotiable hours (sleep, hygiene, meals - let's estimate this at 70 hours per week for simplicity).

4. **Planning : **
   A. Allocate hours to work and study, as these are the most rigid.
   B. Then insert yoga and painting, placing these activities in slots where they can bring the most relaxation and balance.
   C. Be sure to set aside blocks of time for personal study.
   D. Allocate the remaining hours for rest, social and personal activities.

5. **Creating a weekly schedule: ** Having functionally allocated hours, Emma can now create a visual schedule of her week, including blocks of time for each priority

activity.

6. **Review and adjustment:** After a few weeks, Emma needs to review her schedule to adjust what's working and what's not. Perhaps some activities are taking longer than expected, or she realizes she needs more relaxation time.

**Exercise conclusion : **

This exercise will help Emma visualize where and how she spends her time, enabling her to identify opportunities for optimization to better balance her obligations and leisure time. Effective time management doesn't mean doing everything, but doing what matters most in an efficient and enjoyable way.

Conclusion

Banks remain indispensable pillars of the economy, facilitating financial exchanges and supporting economic development. Understanding how they operate, their services and regulation is key to navigating the financial world effectively. Despite the challenges posed by technological innovation and growing competition from fintechs, banks continue to evolve to meet the changing needs of their customers.

Chapter 8. Personal finance

Managing personal finances is a crucial aspect of everyone's life, as it directly influences our quality of life, our financial security and our ability to achieve our long-term goals.

To manage your personal finances effectively, it's essential to establish a financial strategy tailored to your goals, means and priorities. Here are a few tips to help you manage your personal finances more effectively:

1. Establish a Budget

- **Track Income and Expenses**: Knowing your monthly income and expenses enables you to create a realistic budget and manage your money effectively.

- Define Expense Categories**: Allocate funds for essential expenses (housing, food, bills) as well as savings, leisure and discretionary spending.

2. Saving and Investing

- **Emergency Fund**: Save enough to cover at least three to six months of expenses in case of unforeseen circumstances.

- Invest for the Future**: Explore investment options such as savings accounts, index funds, stocks or RRSPs to grow your money over the long term.

3. Reduce Debt

- **Priority Debt Repayment**: Focus on repaying high-interest debt first to reduce long-term costs.

- Debt Consolidation**: Explore options such as debt consolidation to simplify payments and reduce interest.

3. Saving and Investing

- **Emergency Fund**: Set aside an amount of money equivalent to several months' expenses to deal with unforeseen situations.

- Save Regularly**: Set a percentage of your income to save each month, and automate your transfers to your savings account.

- **Explore Investment Options**: Learn about the different investment options available and diversify your portfolio to optimize your returns.

4. Financial Education

Learn and Train: Improve your financial knowledge by reading books, taking online courses, or consulting professionals to better understand financial concepts and make informed decisions.

5. Regular Monitoring and Review

- **Regularly Monitor Your Budget**: Review your budget each month to monitor your progress, adjust if necessary, and stay on track.

- Review Your Financial Goals**: Periodically re-evaluate your financial goals based on your needs, priorities and changes in your financial situation.

By applying these principles of personal financial management, you can build a solid foundation for long-term financial health. The key lies in planning, discipline, regularity and knowledge of your finances.

to take control of your financial future and achieve your financial goals.

Case **study:

Julia, 29, works as a freelance graphic designer. Although she earns enough to cover her monthly expenses, she finds it difficult to save for her long-term goals, such as buying her first home and preparing for retirement. After examining her finances, here's what she discovers:

- Monthly income (after tax): €3000

- Monthly fixed expenses (rent, insurance, subscriptions): €1500

- Variable expenses (food, entertainment, unforeseen events): €800

She realizes that she could potentially put aside €700 each month, but she hasn't yet put a plan in place to do so effectively.

**Financial year : **

1. **Initial financial balance sheet: ** Julia needs to start by creating a clear financial balance sheet. This involves listing her assets (savings, investments, property) and liabilities (debts, loans). She discovers that she has €5,000 in savings and no significant debt.

2. **Setting financial goals: ** Julia decides to set clear short-, medium- and long-term goals. In the short term (1 year), she wants to

build up an emergency fund of €3,000. In the medium term (3 years), she plans to invest €5,000 in a diversified portfolio. In the long term (10 years), her goal is to buy a house.

3. **Create a budget:** To reach her goals, Julia needs to establish a monthly budget, allocating her resources strategically. She decides to reduce her variable expenses to €600, saving €900 a month.

4. **Savings plan :** With €900 available for savings, here's how she can allocate that money:

- €500 in a savings account dedicated to the emergency fund until it reaches €3,000.

- 200 € in a medium-term investment plan.
- 200 in a home savings account for her house.

5. **Reassessment and adjustment :** Every 6 months, Julia should reassess her

finances. This involves adjusting her budget in line with changes in her income and expenses, assessing progress towards her financial goals, and readjusting her savings contributions if necessary.

**Conclusion of exercise : **

This exercise highlights the importance of taking stock of your finances, setting clear objectives and drawing up an appropriate budget and savings plan. It also shows the need to remain flexible and adjust your plan as your financial situation evolves.

Chapter 9. Continuous learning

Lifelong learning is a dynamic, evolving process that involves constant commitment to acquiring new knowledge, skills and perspectives throughout life.

It's a proactive approach to stimulating personal and professional growth, fostering adaptability and resilience, and maintaining constant intellectual curiosity. By engaging in a process of continuous learning, individuals cultivate an open mind, seek opportunities for improvement and expand their field of vision to remain relevant and competitive in a constantly changing world.

This commitment to lifelong learning not only fosters individual development, but also contributes to enriching social interactions, strengthening innovation capabilities and promoting a culture of growth and excellence.

Whether on a professional or personal level, engaging in a continuous learning process brings many benefits. Here are just a few reasons why continuous learning is important:

1. Personal development

- **Acquiring New Skills** : Continuous learning enables you to acquire new skills, explore new areas and broaden your horizons.

- **Personal Growth**: By engaging in a constant learning process, you foster personal growth, self-confidence and self-esteem.

2. Professional Benefits

- **Maintaining Relevance**: In a fast-changing professional environment, continuous learning is essential to remain relevant, competitive and adaptable.

- **Career Opportunities**: By enhancing your skills and knowledge, you increase your chances of career advancement and access to new professional opportunities.

3. Adaptability

- **Flexibility**: Continuous learning strengthens your ability to adapt to change, take on new challenges and adjust to developments in the professional and personal world.

- **Resilience**: By cultivating a learning mindset, you develop an attitude of resilience in the face of obstacles, setbacks and unforeseen changes.

4. Mental Stimulation

- **Maintaining Curiosity**: Continuous learning nourishes your intellectual curiosity, stimulates your mind and encourages you to explore new topics and concepts.

- **Preventing Mental Degeneration**: Engaging in stimulating learning activities can help maintain mental health, prevent cognitive degeneration and promote healthy cognition over the long term.

5. Social Contribution

- **Sharing Knowledge** : By learning continuously, you enrich your knowledge and experience, which can enable you to contribute to society by sharing your skills with others.

- **Networking** : Continuous learning can enable you to meet new people, expand your professional and social networks, and benefit from diverse perspectives.

**Case study: **

Sophie is a digital marketing professional with five years' experience. She realizes that the digital marketing sector is evolving rapidly and that new skills, such as data analysis and artificial intelligence (AI) in marketing, are becoming increasingly important. Sophie wants to remain competitive in the job market by mastering these new skills, but is unsure how to fit this continuous learning into her already busy schedule.

Specific data :

- Sophie works 40 hours a week.
- She devotes 10 hours a week to her hobbies and personal obligations.
- Sophie is motivated to devote 5 hours a week to her learning.

Objective: Sophie wants to effectively integrate a continuous learning program into her routine to acquire skills in data analysis and AI applied to digital marketing.

Exercise :

1. **Identify target skills:** Make a list of the specific skills Sophie wants to learn or improve. For example, data analysis with Excel, Google Analytics, basics of artificial

intelligence in marketing.

2. **Resource search:** Search for online courses, webinars, podcasts and books that can help Sophie learn these skills. Prioritize free or low-cost resources available on platforms like Coursera, EdX, LinkedIn Learning, etc.

3. **Learning planning:**
   A. Make a weekly learning plan, strategically allocating 5 hours. For example, an hour every working day, or longer sessions over the weekend.
   B. Set clear, achievable goals for each week and month, bearing in mind that progress in small steps is more manageable and less daunting.

4. **Integration into daily routine:** Sophie might consider times of day when she's most receptive to learning. For example, reading relevant articles over breakfast or listening to podcasts during her jogging routine or while driving to work.

5. **Learning community:** Join online groups or forums related to digital marketing and data analytics to ask questions, share discoveries and stay motivated through a sense of community.

6. **Putting it into practice:** To reinforce her learning, Sophie should look for opportunities, at work or on personal projects, to practice the skills she has learned. Learning by doing is one of the most effective ways of consolidating new knowledge.

7. **Evaluation and adjustment:** Every month, she should assess her progress by asking herself questions such as, "What have I learned?" "How can I apply these skills in my work?" If certain areas need more attention, adjust the plan accordingly.

Exercise conclusion:

This exercise will help Sophie structure her

lifelong learning path realistically and effectively, keeping herself up to date with the latest trends in her industry while balancing her other responsibilities. Continuous learning is key to professional and personal progression, and by following these steps, Sophie can ensure that she remains a competitive and enlightened professional in her field.

In short, lifelong learning is a catalyst for continuous personal and professional growth. It fosters adaptability, curiosity and mental stimulation, and helps maintain a proactive, positive attitude to life's changes and challenges. By engaging in a constant learning process, we invest in our own potential, resilience and long-term well-being.

Chapter 10. The important thing is not how much you earn but how you earn it

The key lies in how you acquire your income, rather than the exact amount you receive. It's crucial to consider how you generate your income, particularly in terms of efficiency, ethics, sustainability and overall impact, beyond just the amount of money you earn. How you choose to earn your money can influence various aspects of your life, such as your personal satisfaction, professional awareness, contribution to society and work-life balance. Ultimately, the value of your income lies not only in the amount, but also in the values, principles and efforts you choose to put into earning it. The process by which you generate your income can reflect your character, motivations and goals, and can play a significant role in your overall well-being and personal fulfillment.

This statement highlights the importance of how you manage your finances, rather than the exact amount you earn. Managing your money effectively, whatever your income, is essential to ensuring your financial stability, achieving your goals and guaranteeing long-term security. Here are a few key points that underline the importance of financial management over and above income:

1. Saving and Investing Wisely

- **Saving for the Future**: No matter how much you earn, the act of saving regularly can help build a financial reserve for emergencies and long-term goals.

- Invest Wisely**: Learning how to invest wisely can help you grow your savings and secure a more stable financial future, no matter how much you start with.

2. Setting Financial Goals

- **Defining Clear Goals**: Having well-defined financial goals and developing a plan to achieve them is crucial, regardless of your income level.

- **Managing Expenses**: Controlling your

expenses, establishing a budget and eliminating unnecessary debt are essential practices for sound financial management, regardless of your income.

3. Financial Literacy

Financial Education: Learning how to effectively manage your finances, invest and maximize your income is a valuable skill that can help you prosper regardless of how much you earn.

4. Attitude towards Money

Responsible Financial Behavior: Cultivating a responsible attitude towards money, based on reflection, informed decision-making and planning, is essential to ensuring a stable financial situation.

In summary, careful management of your finances, long-term planning, regular savings, wise investing and financial education are key elements in ensuring financial stability and maintaining financial health regardless of how much money you earn . Focusing on how you manage your money can have a significant impact on your long-term financial security and well-being.

Managing your finances effectively is essential to your success. Sound financial management can help you achieve your goals, reduce money-related stress and ensure long-term financial stability. Here are some tips on how to manage your money well and improve your chances of success:

1. Establish a Budget

- **Track Income and Expenses**: Knowing your income and expenses allows you to create a realistic budget.
- Prioritize**: Allocate your funds according to what's essential (housing, food) and your long-term financial goals.

2. Saving and Investing

- **Emergency Fund**: Put money aside for the unexpected.

- Investing for the Future**: Explore investment options to grow your savings and achieve your long-term financial goals.

3. Reduce Debt

- **Pay Down Priority Debt**: Focus on the repayment of high-interest debts.
- **Manage Debt*: Find ways to consolidate or negotiate your debts to reduce monthly payments.

4. Plan and Set Goals

- **Set Financial Goals**: Having clear goals motivates you to proactively manage your money.

- Review Regularly**: Review your financial situation periodically to ensure you're making progress towards your goals.

5. Financial Education

Learn and Train: Improve your financial knowledge by reading books, taking online courses, or consulting professionals.

By managing your money responsibly and proactively, you'll be able to take control of your financial future, maximize your opportunities for success, and create a solid foundation for long-term financial stability.

Chapter 11. The desire to succeed

The drive to succeed is a powerful motivator that can push you to pursue your goals, push your limits and make your dreams come true. It's an inner drive that inspires you to use determination, perseverance and courage to achieve success. Here are some key points on the drive to succeed:

1. Determination and Focus

- **Clear Goals**: Having well-defined goals gives you a direction to follow and motivation to persevere.
- Resilience**: The desire to succeed helps you overcome obstacles, learn from setbacks and bounce back stronger.

2. Passion and Commitment

 - **Passion and Interest**: When you're passionate about what you do, the drive to succeed becomes natural.
 - **Commitment**: Commitment to your goals strengthens your resolve to overcome

challenges and stay focused on your success.

3. Learn and Evolve

- **Curiosity and Continuous Improvement**: The desire to succeed drives you to learn, develop and constantly improve.
- Getting out of your Comfort Zone**: To succeed, it's often necessary to get out of your comfort zone and accept challenges.

4. Visualization and Positivity

- **Visualizing Success**: Visualizing your success can boost your motivation and give you the impetus to persevere.

- Positive Thinking**: Adopting a positive, optimistic attitude can help you overcome moments of doubt and stay focused on your goals.

5. Perseverance and Discipline

- **Perseverance**: The desire to succeed gives you the strength to persevere despite challenges and setbacks.
- Discipline**: Discipline is essential to stay focused on your goals, even when motivation wanes.

By cultivating and nurturing your desire to succeed, you strengthen your chances of realizing your aspirations and achieving your goals. It's this inner drive that pushes you to surpass yourself, to believe in your abilities and to pursue your path to success with determination.

Absolutely, the desire to succeed is one of the keys to success. This inner strength, deep motivation and burning desire to achieve one's goals play a crucial role in achieving great things. Here's how the desire to succeed can be one of the keys to success:

1. Motivation and Determination

- **Intrinsic Motivation** : The desire to succeed comes from within, it's a powerful motor that drives you to act and persevere.

- Determination**: This burning desire gives you the mental and emotional strength to overcome obstacles and stay focused on your goals.

2. Vision and Goal Clarity

- **Clear Vision**: The drive to succeed helps you visualize your success and stay focused on your long-term vision.

- Definite Goals**: It pushes you to set clear, achievable goals, enabling you to make significant progress.

3. Perseverance and Resilience

- **Perseverance**: When you have a strong desire to succeed, you're more likely to persevere despite obstacles and setbacks.

- Resilience**: This drive helps you bounce back from setbacks, learn from your experiences and move forward with determination.

4. Energy and Commitment

- **Positive Energy**: The desire to succeed fuels your energy and gives you the strength you need to invest fully in your projects.

- Total Commitment**: You're more likely to commit fully to what you do when you have a strong desire to succeed, which fosters achievement and excellence.

5. Personal Growth

- **Seeking Improvement**: This drive to succeed drives you to continually seek to improve yourself, learn new skills and broaden your horizons.
- **Self-Expansion**: It encourages you to step out of your comfort zone, take on challenges and aim for ambitious goals,

which contributes to your personal and professional growth.

Case study: Léa's desire to succeed in the fashion industry

Léa is a young fashion designer who recently graduated from a prestigious design school. Passionate about sustainable fashion, she has always dreamed of launching her own brand that would promote ethical and ecological practices in the industry. However, despite her talent and motivation, Léa sometimes feels discouraged when faced with the many challenges of the entrepreneurial world.

**Situation and objectives : **

- Launch a sustainable fashion brand with an initial collection of 10 pieces
- Find financing for the production and marketing of her collection
- Create an online presence and reach 1000

followers on social networks within the first 3 months. **Challenges : **

- Lack of financial resources for large-scale production
- Highly competitive fashion market
- Need to develop digital marketing skills

**Strategy for overcoming challenges and realizing dream: **

1. **Networking and Mentoring: ** Léa decides to actively participate in fashion and sustainability events to expand her network. She is also looking for a mentor with experience in launching sustainable fashion brands.

2. **Crowdfunding: ** To make up for her lack of funds, Léa launches a crowdfunding campaign, highlighting her brand's unique story and its mission to promote sustainable fashion.

3. **Online presence:** She invests time in creating a strong online presence, starting with social networks where she shares her creative process, the story behind each piece, and the importance of sustainable fashion.

4. **Collaborations:** Léa partners with other emerging designers and influencers in the sustainable fashion niche to increase her visibility.

5. **Continuous learning:** Aware of her shortcomings in digital marketing, she enrolls in online courses to acquire the skills needed to effectively promote her brand.

Target outcome: By adopting a strategic approach and staying true to her values, Léa hopes not only to launch her first collection successfully, but also to lay the foundations for an eco-friendly fashion brand recognized for its commitment to sustainability.

This case highlights the importance of having the drive to succeed, not only by having a clear vision but also by being prepared to overcome challenges through perseverance, innovation and continuous learning.

Roughly speaking, the desire to succeed is a powerful driving force that can propel you towards success by providing you with the motivation and determination to achieve your goals. By nurturing this drive, staying focused on your vision and working with perseverance, you maximize your chances of succeeding in your endeavors and achieving great accomplishments.

Chapter 12. The keys to success

The question of how to succeed is a universal one, and one that gives rise to a variety of reflections. The concept of success can vary from person to person, depending on personal goals, values and aspirations. However, some general principles and strategies can be applied to increase the chances of success in various areas of life.

Keys to success could cover many subjects, being a broad theme relevant to many areas of life such as studies, professional careers, personal projects and relationships.

Introduction

The introduction highlights the importance of success in various aspects of life, emphasizing that success is not just limited to professional or academic achievements, but also extends to personal accomplishments and rewarding relationships. It asks a fundamental question: What defines success for each and every one of us?

Here are some key points to consider for success:

1. Define Your Definition of Success

- **Clarify Your Goals**: Identify what constitutes success for you, whether professionally, personally, financially, or emotionally.

- **Set Clear Goals**: Define concrete, measurable and achievable
goals to guide your actions and decisions.

2. Develop Skills and Knowledge

- **Continuous Learning**: Pursue lifelong learning to acquire new skills and stay relevant in a fast-changing world.

- **Develop Your Strengths**: Identify your strengths and work to develop them further to maximize your potential.

3. Build Positive Relationships

- **Networking**: Cultivate strong professional and personal relationships to benefit from the support, advice and opportunities they offer.

- **Entourage Inspiring People**: Associate with people who motivate, encourage and challenge you.

4. Demonstrate Perseverance and Resilience

- **Take Action**: Implement concrete action plans to make progress towards your goals, even in the face of obstacles.

- **Learn from Adversity**: Face failures and challenges as opportunities for learning and personal growth.

5. Maintain Balance and Well-Being

- **Life Balance**: Make sure you maintain a healthy balance between your different spheres of life: work, family, leisure, health.

- **Preserve Your Well-Being**: Take care of your physical, mental and emotional health to be at your best.

Ultimately, success is a personal and unique process that involves defining your goals, acquiring skills, persevering in the face of challenges and cultivating positive relationships. By following these general principles and staying true to yourself, you give yourself the best chance of succeeding in whatever you undertake.

To succeed, it's important to adopt strategies and habits that encourage progress towards your goals. Here are a few recommendations to increase your chances of success:

1. Set Clear, Realistic Goals

- Identify your specific goals and determine the steps needed to achieve them.
- Make sure your goals are measurable, achievable and relevant to motivate you.

2. Plan and Organize

- Establish a detailed action plan with deadlines and milestones to track your progress.
- Prioritize your tasks and manage your time effectively to maximize your productivity.

3. Develop Skills and Knowledge

- Invest in your personal and professional development by acquiring new skills and enriching your knowledge.
- Be open to continuous learning and self-improvement to remain competent and adaptable.

4. Demonstrate Perseverance and Resilience

- Accept setbacks and failures as opportunities for learning and growth rather than insurmountable obstacles.
- Remain persistent, patient and determined even in the face of challenges and difficult times.

5. Establish Positive Relationships

- Surround yourself with people who support, inspire and encourage you to achieve your goals.

- Cultivate strong professional and personal relationships that contribute to your success and fulfillment.

6. Take Care of Yourself

- Give importance to your physical, mental and emotional
well-being by adopting healthy lifestyle habits.

- Maintain a balance between work and personal life, and make sure you take time to recharge and relax.

By following these tips and putting them into practice, you increase your chances of succeeding in your endeavours and achieving your goals. Success is often the result of a combination of determination, planning, perseverance and personal development, coupled with a positive, proactive approach to challenges.

Case study: Keys to Success for Thomas, Entrepreneur in the Making

Thomas, a young entrepreneur with a passion for technology, wants to launch his own startup in the field of artificial intelligence. Convinced that perseverance, creativity and networking are essential keys to success in his business, Thomas sets himself ambitious goals to make his dream of a successful startup a reality.

**Objectives and Keys to Success for Thomas : **

1. **Strategic vision : ** Thomas develops a detailed strategic plan for his startup, clearly defining its value proposition, target audience, short- and long-term goals, and growth strategy.

2. **Creativity and Innovation: ** He cultivates his creativity by collaborating with AI experts, following the latest technological trends, and exploring innovative solutions to industry problems.

3. **Perseverance and Discipline:** Aware of the challenges ahead, Thomas adopts a perseverance and discipline mentality. He remains determined to overcome obstacles and learn from setbacks to move forward to success.

4. **Networking and Collaboration:** Thomas joins startup incubators, technology events and discussion groups to expand his professional network, find mentors and potential partners, and benefit from sound advice to guide his growth.

Strategies Implemented:

1. **Product development:** Thomas is working on an innovative AI prototype, gathering feedback from users and iterating rapidly to improve his product in line with market needs.

2. **Marketing and Communication:** He develops a targeted digital marketing

strategy to promote his startup, using social media, content marketing and SEO to increase visibility and generate qualified leads.

3. **Fundraising : **To ensure the growth of his startup, Thomas explores funding opportunities by participating in startup competitions, pitching to investors and seeking government grants to support his vision.

4. **Monitoring and Adaptability: ** Thomas keeps a close eye on his startup's performance, analyzing key metrics, listening to customer feedback and being ready to adjust his strategy as the market evolves.

**Expected Outcome: ** By putting these keys to success into practice and working with determination, Thomas aims to make his startup a major player in the AI industry, create a positive impact through innovative technological solutions, and become an inspirational leader for aspiring entrepreneurs.

This real-life case highlights the importance of keys to success such as strategic vision, creativity, perseverance, networking and adaptability, which can guide an entrepreneur towards success in achieving his or her professional and personal goals.

Chapter 13. Daring to take on challenges

Daring to take the plunge is a crucial step towards achieving your goals and realizing your aspirations. It's the first step towards realizing your dreams, and the beginning of a journey towards success.

Daring to take the plunge is often the essential starting point for success. Indeed, as the saying goes, "nothing ventured, nothing gained", it's important to overcome your fears, and take calculated risks to achieve your goals.

Daring to take the plunge and rise to the challenge are courageous actions that can pave the way to new opportunities, personal growth and success.

By confronting the unknown, stepping out of your comfort zone and facing challenges with determination, you demonstrate an inner strength and boldness that can lead to remarkable achievements.

Here are a few points to keep in mind to encourage you to dare to launch yourself towards success:

1. identify your fears

- **Identify your fears**: Take a moment to think about the fears or doubts that are holding you back.
- Understand Your Reasons**: Analyze why you feel this fear and what obstacles are preventing you from taking action.

- Overcoming Apprehension**: Taking the plunge often involves facing fears and doubts that can hold you back.
- Accepting Uncertainty**: Acknowledging and accepting uncertainty is the key to success.

part of the process of meeting a challenge.

2. Visualize Your Success

- **Visualize Your Goal**: Imagine

yourself achieving your goal and feeling the positive emotions associated with that success.

- Focus on the Benefits**: Concentrate on the advantages and opportunities you could seize by taking the plunge.

3. Take Small Actions

- **Start Small**: Break down your goal into smaller, more achievable steps.

- Take a First Step**: Identify one simple action you can take right now to get closer to your goal.

4. Cultivate a Positive Mentality
- **Adopt a Positive Attitude**: Replace negative thoughts with constructive and encouraging ones.
- Believe in Yourself**: Have confidence in your abilities and potential to succeed.

- **Believe in your Abilities**: Self confidence is essential if you are to dare to

venture into the unknown.
- Recognizing your Strengths**: Identifying your strengths and resources can boost your confidence in meeting challenges.

5. Get out of Your Comfort Zone
 - **Accept the Risk**: Accept that there is an element of uncertainty and risk associated with the start of any project.
- Challenge Your Limits**: Progress and personal growth lie beyond your comfort zone.

6. Accept Failure as Part of the Path

- **Learn from Failure**: Consider failure as a necessary learning step towards success.
- Bounce Back**: Bounce back from failure and use the experience to move forward.

7. Accept Risk

- **Take Calculated Risks**: Daring to take the plunge means taking measured risks and

getting out of your comfort zone.
- **Learn from Experience**: Challenges can be opportunities for learning and personal growth, even in the face of failure.

8. The Possibility of Realizing Your Dreams

- By overcoming your fears and taking risks, you're one step closer to realizing your deepest dreams and aspirations.
- Taking the plunge can set you on the path to success, helping you turn your goals into reality and make significant progress in your life.

9. Personal fulfillment

- Daring to take on stimulating challenges can lead to a sense of accomplishment and personal pride.
- By enabling you to explore new horizons, develop your self-confidence and push back your limits, you promote personal fulfillment.

By daring to take the plunge, overcoming your fears and taking positive action, you'll create positive momentum towards achieving your goals. Taking the plunge requires courage, determination and self-confidence, but this boldness can open the door to opportunities and successes you'd never have imagined otherwise.

Case study: Daring to take the plunge and rise to the challenge for Sofia, Aspiring Entrepreneur

Sofia has been working in the digital marketing sector for several years, but feels a deep calling to launch her own marketing agency to support small local businesses in their digital strategy. Although she had the necessary experience and skills, fear of failure and financial challenges prevented her from taking the plunge. However, she finally decided to take action and make her entrepreneurial dream come true.

**Sofia's objectives and challenges : **

1. **Objective - Start her own marketing agency: ** Create an agency specializing in digital marketing for small businesses with personalized customer service and innovative solutions.

2. **Challenges : **
Overcome fear of failure and self-doubt.
   - Managing the financial risks of starting your own business.

   - Acquire new customers and establish credibility in the marketplace: **

1. **Market Research and Business Plan: ** Sofia conducts an in-depth analysis of the local market, identifies her target clientele and creates a detailed business plan to guide the development of her agency.

2. **Idea validation: ** Before fully launching, Sofia conducts pilot tests and gathers feedback from potential customers to

validate her concept and adjust her offer accordingly.

3. **Skills enhancement :** To feel more confident in her role as a manager, Sofia takes training courses in business management, leadership and strategic marketing to acquire the skills she needs to make her business a success.

4. **Networking and Mentoring:** Sofia joins local entrepreneurial networks, participates in networking events and actively seeks out an experienced mentor for practical advice and emotional support.

**Exercise - Stepping out of her Comfort Zone: **

1. **List of Fears and Obstacles: ** Sofia specifically identifies the fears and obstacles that prevent her from taking the plunge, then ranks them in order of importance.

2. **Setting achievable objectives: ** She sets SMART (Specific, Measurable,

Attainable, Realistic, Time-bound) goals for each stage of her business start-up process, starting with simpler goals and progressing to more ambitious ones.

3. **Gradual Action Plan:** Sofia creates a step-by-step action plan, dividing her tasks into achievable steps and planning concrete actions to overcome her fears and meet the challenges ahead.

4. **Putting it into Practice:** She begins to step out of her comfort zone by taking courageous actions and small challenges every day, gradually getting used to taking risks and dealing with uncertainty.

5. **Self-evaluation and adjustment:** Sofia regularly reviews her progress, reflects on lessons learned, celebrates her successes and adjusts her action plan based on new discoveries and experiences.

Through this exercise, Sofia learns to face her fears, take calculated risks and overcome the challenges that stand in her way to realize her entrepreneurial dream. By daring to take the plunge step by step and facing obstacles with determination, Sofia strengthens her self-confidence and her ability to overcome challenges strategically and perseveringly.

Chapter 14. Generating income with small amounts of capital

Creating income with a small amount of capital is a challenge that many people aspire to take up, whether to supplement their main income, to build wealth or simply to test their entrepreneurial flair.

Investing with small capital may seem tricky, but it's actually a great way to enter the world of investing and start building your assets. Here are some practical tips from the experts to help you maximize your small investment capital

Introduction

The introduction to this chapter could state the importance of creativity and determination in the process of generating income from a small amount of capital. It could also highlight the digital age in which we live, which offers unprecedented opportunities for those who are willing to learn and adapt.

Understanding the potential of your capital

Initially, it is crucial to make an honest assessment of the capital available, both in time and money. This section could discuss ways of increasing this initial capital, either through savings, or through secondary activities that can generate additional income.

The choice of initial investment

1. **Investing in the stock market with limited funds:** Presentation of investment platforms that allow you to start with small amounts, while explaining the basics of stock market investing, including fractional shares.
2. **Launching a dropshipping e-commerce business:** Explaining how to start a dropshipping business with little money, focusing on niche research, choosing suppliers, and using platforms like Shopify

or WooCommerce to build an e-commerce site.

3. **Digital content creation:** Discuss how to monetize your passion or expertise through the creation of blogs, podcasts, or YouTube videos. Emphasize the importance of SEO, regular content, and audience engagement strategies.

Using personal skills

This section could explore how to use specific skills or talents to generate income. Some ideas:
- Freelance writing or graphic design on platforms like Fiverr or Upwork.
- Online courses or video tutorials on subjects of expertise, sold through platforms like Udemy or Teachable.
- Personal coaching or consulting in specialized niches.

Establish an online presence

Emphasize the importance of a strong online presence to the success of almost any revenue-generating initiative. This could include the creation of a professional website, the use of social networking sites, etc.

for marketing and building a personal brand.

Reinvest dividends

- **Reinvest your earnings :** If your investments pay dividends, consider reinvesting them. This can help accelerate your portfolio's growth without requiring you to invest additional equity.

Be patient and consistent

- **Patience and consistency :** Investing is a marathon, not a sprint. Being patient and consistent with your investments can lead to significant growth over the long term, even if your initial capital is small.

By following these tips, you can effectively start investing and generating income even with a small amount of capital. The important thing is to get started, be strategic in your choices, and engage in a continuous learning process to maximize your chances of success.

Let's imagine the story of Lucie, a young professional who has saved 1,000 euros and wants to use this capital to generate additional income. With a limited budget, Lucie needs to use her creativity and ingenuity to invest wisely.

Step 1: Assessment and Planning

Lucie starts by assessing her skills, passions and available resources. She is gifted in graphic design and has a passion for interior design. Lucie decides to use her capital to launch a small business designing visuals for social media, specifically targeting small businesses and entrepreneurs in the interior design sector.

Step 2: Minimal Investment in Necessary Tools

With part of her capital, Lucie buys a monthly subscription to graphic design software and invests in promoting her services on social networks and freelance platforms. She uses free online templates and customizes them to create unique, eye-catching visuals.

Step 3: Creating an Online Portfolio

To attract customers, Lucie knows she needs to showcase her best creations. She spends time building an online portfolio using a free website creation service. She includes samples of her work, testimonials from satisfied customers, and clear information on how to contact her for orders.

Step 4: Networking and Promotion

Lucie uses social networks to connect with entrepreneurs and small business owners in interior design. She regularly shares her creations and participates in conversations to increase her visibility. In addition, she invests a small amount in targeted advertising on social networks to reach a wider audience.

Step 5: Diversification and Reinvestment

After the first few months, Lucie starts to get regular customers and her income gradually increases. She reinvests part of her earnings to subscribe to online courses that could improve her design skills. In addition, Lucie explores new market niches and expands her offerings to include packaging design and branding for small businesses.

Step 6: Scalability

Over time, demand for Lucie's services grows. She decides to gradually increase her rates while maintaining the high quality of her work. At the same time, she begins to outsource certain tasks to other freelancers so that she can take on more projects without sacrificing her quality of life.

Conclusion

Starting from just 1,000 euros, Lucie has managed to create a steady stream of additional income by leveraging her existing skills and investing wisely in the promotion of her services. Her story illustrates how, with a little creativity and a lot of determination, it's possible to generate additional income even with a small start-up capital.

I encourage you to remain flexible, to adapt to market changes, and not to fear failure, because every mistake is a valuable lesson on the road to success.

Case study: Creating income with a small amount of capital for Max, aspiring entrepreneur.

Max is a student with a passion for developing mobile applications, but he has a limited budget to invest in his own.

business project. Despite financial constraints, he is determined to find creative ways to generate revenue and grow his business prudently.

**Max's Objectives and Constraints: **

1. **Objective - Create Income with Small Capital: ** Start a profitable mobile app development business using limited resources efficiently.

2. **Constraints : **
Limited initial capital for investments.

- Need to find innovative strategies to generate revenue and grow the business sustainably.

**Strategies Implemented : **

1. **Use of Free Resources: **
- Max explores free and open-source development platforms to minimize the initial costs of creating applications.

- He relies on free design tools and online tutorials to improve his skills without having to invest in expensive training.

2. **Creative Business Model: **
- Max is developing a monthly subscription-based business model for its apps, offering premium features in exchange for recurring payment from users.
- It is also exploring partnerships with local businesses to integrate sponsored features into its applications in exchange for commissions or advertising payments.

3. **Low-Cost Marketing:**
- Max focuses on low-cost digital marketing, using social media, organic SEO and content marketing to promote his apps effectively without spending huge sums on advertising.

- He relies on word-of-mouth marketing, encouraging satisfied early adopters to recommend his apps to their network.

Exercise - Maximizing Available Resources :

1. **Skills and Assets Assessment:** Max identifies his key skills and the resources he already possesses, such as his knowledge of application development, his personal network, and his marketing skills.

2. **Market Needs Analysis:** He conducts market research to identify unmet needs in the mobile app sector, and selects a lucrative niche where his skills can be put to good use.

3. **Setting an Accurate Budget:** Max establishes a realistic budget by determining the initial costs required to launch his business, and identifying areas where savings can be made.

4. **Creating a Step-by-Step Action Plan:** He develops a detailed action plan by setting progressive objectives, determining the key steps to achieve these objectives, and defining the resources required at each stage.

5. **Results Measurement and Constant Adjustment:** Max monitors

closely monitor the performance of his applications, analyze user data, and adjust his strategy based on feedback to optimize revenue and growth.

This exercise helps Max make the most of his limited resources, find ingenious ways to generate revenue, and grow his business profitably despite his small start-up capital. By focusing on efficiency, creativity and sustainable growth, Max lays the foundations for a successful and resilient business. This chapter, while providing concrete paths to getting started with little capital, could be enhanced with testimonials, case studies, and expert advice to motivate and guide you through your entrepreneurial journey.

Chapter 15. Learning to invest

The introduction to this chapter could emphasize the importance of investing in building a solid financial future. It could explain how smart investing can make your money work for you, rather than just work for money.

Understanding the basics of investing

1. **The different types of investment : ** Explain the differences between stocks, bonds, real estate, mutual funds, etc. Present the risks and returns associated with each investment category.
2. **Determine your investor profile: ** Discuss the different investor profiles, risk management, and the importance of defining clear objectives before starting to invest.

Study the different investment strategies

1. **Long-term vs. short-term investing: ** Explain the differences and advantages of

each approach, highlighting the effect of duration on returns.

2. **Investing in individual stocks vs. investment funds:** Compare the two approaches, highlighting the diversification benefits that investment funds offer.

Learn to analyze investments

1. **Fundamental analysis vs. technical analysis :** Explain the basics of these two analysis approaches and how they can be used to make informed investment decisions.

2. **Assessing a company's growth potential:** Introduce the key financial indicators to watch and the key factors to consider when analyzing a company.

Managing an investment portfolio

This section could address practical questions about managing a portfolio, including asset allocation, regular portfolio review, managing gains and losses, and rebalancing strategies.

Avoiding common pitfalls

It would be important to include a section on the most common mistakes made by novice investors, such as lack of diversification, market timing, or panicking in the face of market fluctuations.

Claire, a young professional aged 30, earns a comfortable living, but until recently had never seriously considered investing her money. Her savings were limited to a traditional savings account, with interest so minimal she didn't even notice it. Inspired by the desire to prepare for her financial future and perhaps take early retirement, Claire decides it's time to learn how to invest.

Step 1: Establish her financial goals

Claire starts by clearly defining her investment objectives. She wants to build a portfolio that will enable her to take a comfortable retirement at age 60, while still having an emergency fund for medium-term life projects, such as buying a house or financing future children's education.

Step 2: Assessing her risk tolerance

With a 30-year investment horizon for retirement, Claire is prepared to accept a moderate level of risk to achieve better returns. For her medium-term goals, she opts for less risky options to protect her capital.

Step 3: Financial education

Claire embarks on a process of financial education. She reads books on the basics of investing, takes online courses, and familiarizes herself with key terms like "diversification", "stocks", "bonds", and "index funds". She also learns how to analyze investment options, examining their growth potential, associated risks, and their suitability for her financial goals.

Step 4: Choosing an investment strategy

Armed with the knowledge she has acquired, Claire decides to adopt a long-term investment strategy focused on index funds and ETFs for her retirement, prioritizing diversification while minimizing fees. For her medium-term objectives, she opts for government bonds and high-yield savings accounts.

Step 5: Implementation

Claire opens an online brokerage account and transfers part of her savings to it. She schedules automatic transfers

from her current account to her brokerage account to invest regularly in her chosen funds. For her medium-term objectives, she opens a dedicated savings account with a competitive interest rate.

Step 6: Monitoring and adjustment

Every six months, Claire reassesses her investments. She checks her portfolio's performance, the suitability of her asset allocation with her objectives and her risk tolerance. She adjusts her investments if necessary to stay in line with her financial objectives.

A year after starting to invest, Claire is amazed at how much she has already learned and how much her investment portfolio has grown. She knows she still has a lot to learn, but feels confident that she has taken control of her financial future. Most importantly, she has begun to take proactive steps towards her goals, armed with the knowledge she continues to acquire about investing.

To become an informed and successful investor, it's essential to adopt a disciplined and enlightened approach. Here are some practical tips from investment experts that can help any investor, from beginner to seasoned veteran, improve their skills and maximize their chances of success.

1. Continually educate yourself

- **Read books, articles, and listen to podcasts on investing.** There are a multitude of resources available to help you understand the basics of investing and keep abreast of market trends.

2. Understand your risk profile
- **Make regular assessments of your risk tolerance.** Your financial situation and risk attitude can change. Make sure your investments always reflect your ability to tolerate losses.

3. Diversify your portfolio

- Don't put all your eggs in one basket. ** Investing in a variety of assets can reduce your overall risk. Diversification can include different sectors, geographic areas and asset classes (stocks, bonds, real estate, etc.).

4. Take a long-term view

- **Be patient and avoid emotional reactions. ** Financial markets are volatile in the short term, but tend to grow over the long term. Resist the temptation to sell during a market downturn; often, staying invested is more profitable.

5. Use automation to your advantage

- **Set up automatic transfers to your investment accounts. ** Investing regularly, a concept known as "dollar-cost averaging", can lessen the impact of market volatility on your portfolio.

6. Keep an eye on investment fees

**Beware of management fees and commissions. **

Fees can significantly reduce your long-term returns. Go to

for low-cost investment options, such as index funds and ETFs.

7. Have a plan and follow it

**Define a clear investment plan based on your financial goals and timetable. ** Re-evaluate and adjust your plan as necessary, but avoid impromptu decisions in response to market fluctuations.

8. Keep an emergency fund

**Make sure you have a liquid emergency fund. ** Investing with money you may need in the short term can lead to hasty selling decisions in the event of a financial emergency.

9. Keep abreast of economic and financial news

**Follow global economic and financial

events. ** Even if you adopt a passive investment approach, understanding the global economic context can help you make more informed decisions.

10. Consider professional help

**Ask for a meeting with a financial advisor. ** If you feel overwhelmed by planning and managing your investments, a professional can offer advice tailored to your personal situation.

By adopting these practices, you increase your chances of developing a solid, resilient investment portfolio, capable of

withstand the ups and downs of the market while generating significant long-term returns.

Case study: Learning to invest for Laura, a young professional

Laura is an ambitious young professional

who wants to start investing to ensure her long-term financial stability. With little experience in investing, she is looking to learn the basics to make informed decisions and develop a solid financial portfolio.

**Objectives and Background for Laura : **

1. **Objective - Learn to Invest: ** Acquire basic investment knowledge, define clear financial goals, and begin building a diversified investment portfolio.

2. **Background: **
Laura's limited investment knowledge.

 - Stable income enabling her to start investing regularly.

**Strategies implemented : **

1. **Training and resources: **
- Laura starts by reading investment books, taking online courses, and listening to

financial podcasts to familiarize herself with key concepts and investment strategies.

- She enrolls in local financial workshops, meets with financial advisors, and uses online tools to simulate investment opportunities. Investments and understand the different types of financial instruments.

2. **Defining investment objectives : **
Laura establishes clear short-, medium- and long-term financial goals, such as building an emergency fund, saving for a house, and preparing for retirement.

   - She determines her risk profile, time horizon and investment preferences to guide her investment decisions.

3. **Portfolio diversification : **
- Laura learns to diversify her portfolio by investing in different types of assets, such as stocks, bonds, mutual funds, and commodities, to reduce risk and maximize potential returns.

- It follows a progressive approach, starting with safer, lower-risk investments, before exploring more complex and dynamic options.

Exercise - Step by Step to Investing :

1. **Current Financial Situation Analysis:** Laura assesses her current financial situation, including income, expenses, debts and long-term goals, to determine her readiness to start investing.

2. **Identifying Investment Options:** She researches the various investment options available, examining their advantages, disadvantages and minimum requirements to decide which ones best match her objectives and risk profile.

3. **Setting an Investment Budget :** Laura establishes a monthly or periodic investment budget taking into account her available income and overall financial plan to ensure a sustainable and consistent approach.

4. **Performance monitoring and re-evaluation:** She closely monitors the performance of her investments, analyzes market trends, and periodically re-evaluates her investment decisions based on the evolution of her objectives and her appetite for risk.

5. **Continuing education:** Laura is committed to continuing her financial education, staying informed of new market trends and investment opportunities, and adjusting her strategy accordingly to optimize her long-term returns.

By following this step-by-step exercise, Laura can gradually acquire the skills needed to invest wisely, achieve her financial goals, and build a solid, prosperous financial future.

Conclusion

Conclude by summarizing the key points

covered in the chapter, emphasizing the importance of ongoing education, patience, and discipline in the investment process.

I encourage you to start small, learn from your mistakes, and stay true to your long-term goals.

Chapter 16. Cryptocurrencies, dividends, gold

Investing is a vast and diverse field, offering multiple vehicles for growing one's wealth. Among them, crypto-currencies, dividends from equities, and gold present distinct characteristics, benefits and risks that can attract different types of investors depending on their objectives and risk tolerance. Let's take a look at each of these three types of investment:

Cryptocurrencies

Cryptocurrencies are digital assets designed to function as a medium of exchange that uses strong cryptography to secure financial transactions, control the creation of new units, and verify the transfer of assets. Bitcoin, the first and best-known cryptocurrency, was launched in 2009. Since then, thousands of other cryptocurrencies have been created.

Advantages :

- **High return potential:** Some cryptocurrencies have seen their value increase dramatically over short periods.
- **Liquidity:** Cryptocurrency markets operate 24/7, offering high liquidity.
- **Innovation:** Investing in blockchain technology and cryptocurrencies means investing in a disruptive technology.

Risks :

- **Volatility:** Cryptocurrency prices can experience huge fluctuations in a short space of time.
- **Regulation:** The regulatory environment surrounding cryptocurrencies is still in development, which could introduce additional risks.
- **Security :** Digital assets are susceptible to hacking and fraud if not properly secured.

Dividends

Dividends represent a portion of a company's profits paid out to its shareholders, usually on a quarterly basis. They offer investors a regular income and can be reinvested to buy more shares, harnessing the power of compounding.

**Benefits : **

- **Regular income : **Provides a steady stream of income, which can be particularly attractive for investors seeking passive income or for retirees.
- **Less volatility: ** Companies that pay regular dividends tend to be more stable and less volatile than growth companies that do not pay dividends.
- **Indicator of financial health: ** Regular dividend payments can indicate a company's financial health and fiscal discipline.

**Risks : **

- Dividend cut-off : **In the event of financial difficulties, a company may reduce or eliminate its dividend, thus negatively affecting investors' income.
- **Slower growth: ** Companies that pay dividends potentially reinvest less income in

the company's future growth.

Gold

Gold has been valued by civilizations throughout history for its rarity and beauty, serving as currency, store of value, and investment.

**Benefits : **

- Gold is often considered a safe haven in times of economic crisis or market volatility
- **Hedge against inflation : Historically, gold has maintained its value over time, serving as a hedge against inflation.
** **Diversification: ** Adding gold to a portfolio can help diversify it, reducing overall risk.

**Risks : **

- No income: ** Gold does not generate income such as dividends or interest
- **Storage costs: ** Physical gold requires secure storage, which may entail additional

costs.
- **Volatility:** Although less volatile than cryptocurrencies, the price of gold can still fluctuate wildly.

Each of these types of investment presents a unique set of features, benefits and risks. Crypto-currencies can offer high returns but with significant volatility, dividends provide a steady income with potentially less growth, and gold is a safe haven that nonetheless offers no passive income.

The key to a successful investment portfolio is often diversification, which means that judiciously combining these assets, according to your risk tolerance and investment objectives, can help balance potential reward and risk.

Chapter 17. Real estate companies and subleases

Real estate companies and subleasing can play an essential role in real estate investment strategies. While they offer income-generating opportunities, it's important to understand their dynamics, benefits, and the legal considerations surrounding them.

Real estate companies

Real estate companies, often structured as Sociétés Civiles de Placement Immobilier (SCPIs) or Real Estate Investment Trusts (REITs), allow investors to purchase units or shares representing a stake in diversified real estate portfolios. These entities own, manage or finance income-producing properties.

**Benefits : **

- **Diversification : ** Investors can access a wide range of real estate assets, reducing the risk associated with investing in a single

property.
- **Professional management:** Real estate companies take care of maintenance, tenant management, and administrative aspects.
- **Liquidity:** Shares in REITs, for example, trade on public exchanges, offering more liquidity than direct investment in real estate.

**Considerations : **

- **Market risks: ** The value of real estate companies can be influenced by fluctuations in the real estate and economic markets: ** Management and other fees may reduce the value of your investment returns.

Subletting

Subletting involves renting out a rented property to a third party. For example, a main tenant may sublet all or part of the rental space to a subtenant. This can be attractive for tenants wishing to reduce their rental charges, or for those looking to monetize unused space.

Benefits :

- **Financial flexibility :** Subletting can provide an additional source of income for tenants, helping them to cover some or all of their rent.
- **Efficient use of space:** Allows more efficient use of available space, particularly in areas of high rental demand.

Considerations :
- **Lessor's agreement:** Most rental contracts require the lessor's agreement to allow subletting. Ignoring this requirement can lead to legal consequences
- **Responsibility :** The primary tenant remains responsible for paying rent to the landlord and complying with the original rental agreement, regardless of sub-letting arrangements.
- **Over-occupancy risk:** It is crucial to ensure that subletting does not lead to overuse of the property, which could cause damage or violate local regulations.

Legal and Ethical Aspects

Successful investment in real estate companies or in subletting depends to a large extent on knowledge of and compliance with current laws and regulations. Investors need to familiarize themselves with the legal, tax and regulatory aspects of their investments to avoid costly litigation or financial loss. Investing in real estate companies, including Sociétés Civiles de Placement Immobilier (SCPIs) and Real Estate Investment Trusts (REITs), can be a lucrative strategy for diversifying your investment portfolio while potentially benefiting from regular rental income. Here are some practical tips from experts on how to navigate this aspect of real estate investing:

1. Understanding how SCPIs and REITs work

Before investing, familiarize yourself with the specific mechanisms of SCPIs and REITs. SCPIs operate by acquiring and managing real estate assets, with profits redistributed to shareholders. REITs, which are listed on the stock exchange, enable you to invest in real estate portfolios while benefiting from a certain degree of liquidity.

2. Evaluate the quality of the real estate portfolio

Carefully examine the composition of the real estate company's portfolio. Prefer companies with properties in locations with high growth and profitability potential. Portfolio diversity in terms of property type (office, retail, residential) and geographic location can also be a risk-reducing factor.

3. Analyze historical performance

Although past performance is not a guide to future results, it can be an important indicator of the company's management skills and stability. Check the company's dividend distribution history and the evolution of the value of its shares.

4. Deciphering fees

Real estate companies often charge management and entry fees, which can reduce the overall return on investment. Make sure you understand these costs and compare them with those of other similar companies before making your decision.

5. Study the management strategy

The quality of management is crucial in real estate investment. Analyze the company's acquisition, development and property management strategy. A good real estate company should have a clear strategic vision and demonstrate its ability to adapt to market changes.

6. Beware of promises of high returns

If an investment sounds too good to be true, it probably is. Exceptionally high returns can conceal equally high risks or hidden costs. A cautious approach and investment after careful consideration are recommended.

7. Think long-term

Real estate is traditionally a long-term investment. Market fluctuations can affect the performance of real estate companies in the short term, but a long-term view often helps to smooth out these variations and benefit from long-term growth.

8. Diversify within real estate

Don't put all your eggs in one real estate basket. Investing in different types of SCPIs or REITs, or combining these investments with other types of real estate assets, can help reduce overall risk.

9. Consider tax implications

Income generated by real estate companies may have specific tax implications. Speak to a tax advisor to understand how such income fits into your personal tax situation.

10. Stay informed

Real estate is a constantly evolving market. Stay informed about market trends, regulatory changes and economic factors that can influence the performance of your investments.

By applying these tips, you'll be better prepared to make informed investment choices in real estate companies, maximizing your chances of success while managing the associated risks.

Case study: Investment diversification for Nadia

Nadia is a budding investor looking to develop a diversified financial portfolio to secure her financial future. She is interested in three different asset classes: cryptocurrencies, stock dividends and gold. By exploring different investment options, Nadia seeks to make informed decisions to maximize returns and minimize risk.
 **Nadia's Objectives and Background : **

1. **Objective - Investment Diversification: ** Understand the key aspects of cryptocurrencies, stock dividends and gold, and build a balanced portfolio including these three asset classes.

2. **Context: **
- Nadia is open to learning about new investment opportunities and diversifying her portfolio to minimize risk.

- She wants to maximize her returns while taking into account her risk tolerance and long-term financial goals.

**Strategies Implemented : **

1. **Cryptocurrencies : **

- Nadia begins by familiarizing herself with crypto-currencies, understanding the fundamental concepts of the blockchain, the different types of crypto-currencies and secure exchange platforms.
- She follows the evolution of major crypto-currencies such as Bitcoin and Ethereum, analyzes market trends and develops an investment strategy based on her research and experience. understanding.

2. **Stock Dividends: **
- Nadia studies the different types of

dividend-paying stocks, solid companies offering attractive returns, and how to build a diversified dividend-focused equity portfolio.

- She considers capital growth, dividend yields and company stability before selecting the stocks best suited to her investment strategy.

3. **Gold investment : **
- Nadia explores the benefits of gold as a historic safe-haven asset, the different ways to invest in gold (physical, ETFs, futures, mining companies) and the factors influencing gold prices.

- She evaluates gold as a diversification asset for her portfolio, offering protection against inflation, market volatility and economic crises.

**Exercise - Building a Diversified Portfolio : **

1. **Analysis of investment options : **
Nadia reviews the characteristics, benefits

and risks of cryptocurrencies, stock dividends and gold, identifying how each can contribute to a diversified portfolio.

2. **Defining Financial Objectives:** She clarifies her short- and long-term financial objectives, determines her risk profile and return preferences to guide her investment decisions.

3. **Portfolio allocation:** Nadia considers her ideal portfolio allocation between cryptocurrencies, equity dividends and gold, taking into account her risk tolerance, income targets and growth prospects.

4. **Monitoring and Revaluation:** She regularly monitors the performance of her investments, periodically revising her portfolio strategy in line with market developments and changes in her financial objectives.

By following this exercise, Nadia can build a diversified portfolio drawing on the benefits of each of these asset classes, increasing her chances of success, sustainable growth and long-term financial security.

Conclusion

Investing in real estate companies offers a route to diversification and professional property management, while subletting can provide a flexible strategy for maximizing rental income. However, each approach requires careful attention to legal and financial details, as well as a clear understanding of the obligations and risks involved. As with any form of investment, thorough due diligence and strategic planning are essential.

Chapter 18. Success makes you happy

The relationship between success and happiness is a complex and fascinating subject, often discussed in the field of psychology and personal development. For many people, success is an important factor contributing to their well-being and sense of happiness. Here are some perspectives on how success can influence happiness:

Sense of Achievement

Success, whether professional, personal, or any other field, can be the source of a profound sense of accomplishment. Achieving goals, overcoming obstacles, and seeing oneself progress towards one's aspirations can bring significant personal satisfaction and boost self-esteem.

Impact on Quality of Life

Success can often improve a person's quality of life. This can translate into better access to education, quality healthcare, economic opportunities, and a higher standard of living. These elements can contribute to a person's overall well-being and happiness.

Autonomy and Control

Achieving success can increase a sense of autonomy and control over one's life. This can offer the opportunity to make informed decisions, shape one's own destiny, and play an active role in achieving one's goals.

###Professional or personal success can also have a positive impact on interpersonal relationships. It can strengthen family, friendship and professional ties, foster peer recognition and respect, and contribute to a sense of belonging and social connection.

Balance and fulfillment

Success is measured not only by tangible achievements, but also by a sense of general well-being and personal fulfillment. A balance between the different spheres of life, including work, health, social relationships and leisure, contributes to a successful and fulfilling life.

Perspectives and Goals

Success can also be seen as a motor for personal growth and ongoing development. Achieving a certain level of success can be an incentive to set new challenges, explore new horizons, and continue to grow personally and professionally.

Ultimately, the relationship between success and happiness is subjective and varies from person to person. What's most important is to define your own definitions of success and happiness, taking into account your personal values, priorities and aspirations. Striking a balance between achieving one's goals and maintaining emotional and social well-being can be the key to cultivating a deep sense of happiness and satisfaction in life.

Case study: Balancing Success and Happiness for Marc, Accomplished Entrepreneur

Marc is a successful entrepreneur who founded a successful company in the technology sector. Despite his professional success, he realized that he had become unbalanced, focusing all his energy on his career to the detriment of his personal well-being and family life. Determined to restore the balance between success and happiness, Marc decides to review his priorities and redefine what success really means to him.

**Marc's objectives and background : **
1. **Objective - Balance between Success and Happiness: ** Find a balance between his professional success and his personal happiness, ensuring that his success brings him satisfaction and fulfillment in all aspects of his life.
2. **Background: **
- Marc has experienced rapid growth in his career, but has noticed burnout and a lack of

connection with his family and loved ones.
- He wants to rediscover his passion for entrepreneurship while maintaining a balanced and rewarding life.

**Strategies implemented : **

1. **Redefining Success: **Marc begins by reconsidering his definition of success, incorporating aspects such as well-being, mental health, personal relationships and a sense of personal accomplishment into his assessment of success.

2. **Prioritization : **

He identifies the key areas of his life that deserve his attention, whether career, family, health, leisure or personal development, and prioritizes accordingly.

3. **Time Management and Delegating Responsibilities: **Marc sets
up a more efficient time management

structure, delegating certain professional and personal tasks to lighten his workload and allow himself intervals of rest and recuperation.

4. **Cultivate Well-Being: **

He integrates wellness practices into his daily routine, such as meditation, exercise, reading, nature, taking care of his own emotional and physical well-being.

5. **Strengthen Personal Relationships: **Marc pays
more attention to his family and social relationships, invests quality time with loved ones, and develops authentic bonds to strengthen his network of support and connection.

**Conclusion: **

By adopting these strategies and re-evaluating his vision of success, Marc manages to strike a harmonious balance between his professional success and his personal happiness. He discovers that true success lies not only in external achievements, but also in inner well-being, enriching human relationships and harmony in all aspects of his life. By realigning his priorities and cultivating a lasting balance between success and happiness, Marc is able to lead a more fulfilling and balanced life.

Other success stories:

Successfully raising children is often considered one of the greatest achievements for many parents. Here's why it can be a source of happiness and satisfaction:

Deep Impact

Ensuring that your children grow up balanced, educated and fulfilled can have a profound and lasting impact on their lives. The values, skills and lessons passed on by parents can shape their children's life paths and contribute to their later success.
Parent-Child Relationship

Investing time, energy and love in your children's education often strengthens the bond between them. A solid, positive relationship between parents and children, based on communication, trust and mutual support, can be a source of great satisfaction and happiness for both parties.

Personal fulfillment

Seeing your children succeed, blossom and become responsible adults can be a source of personal fulfillment for parents. Witnessing the milestones in their development, celebrating their successes and seeing them chart their own course in life can be a source of immense pride.

###Well-educated, well-balanced children often have a positive impact on society as a whole. They are more likely to contribute constructively to the community, become engaged citizens and lead ethical and responsible lives.

Legacy and Perennity

The transmission of values, family traditions and education from generation to generation creates a family legacy that can endure long after the parents' lifetime. Knowing that you have sown seeds of wisdom and love that will continue to grow in future generations can be a source of great satisfaction.

Support and Recognition

During the journey of raising children, receiving support and recognition from them can strengthen family bonds. It creates a climate of trust and mutual gratitude that nurtures family happiness.

In short, success in raising your children is much more than just an achievement. It's a deep and meaningful experience that brings indescribable joy, immense gratitude and lasting satisfaction. Parents invest in the future by raising their children, shaping the next generation and contributing to a better, more balanced world.

Successful marriage is a rewarding and meaningful achievement for many couples. Here's why a successful wedding can be a great success:

###A successful marriage often rests on a solid relationship based on trust, respect, communication and mutual support. Cultivating a fulfilling relationship can be a source of happiness and deep satisfaction for spouses.

Personal and mutual growth

Successfully navigating the ups and downs of a couple's relationship can foster personal growth and emotional development. Learning to face challenges together, resolve conflicts and grow as individuals can strengthen the bond between partners.

Sharing Moments of Joy and Difficulty

In a successful marriage, spouses share not only moments of happiness and success, but also trials and difficulties. Overcoming challenges together strengthens the couple's solidarity and togetherness.

Support and Celebration

A successful marriage means offering and receiving unconditional support from your partner. Feeling supported, understood and loved in all circumstances can nurture happiness and fulfillment within the couple.

Model Relationship for Children

A successful marriage can serve as a positive role model for children and their parents. Generations to come. Setting a strong example of partnership, healthy communication and positive conflict resolution can have a lasting impact on family and society.

###Successful marriage often involves a strong commitment to one's partner and an intention to persevere despite challenges. The ability to stay committed, work on the relationship and look to the future together can foster durability and well-being for the couple.

Happiness and fulfillment

A successful marriage can be a source of happiness and fulfillment in everyday life. Sharing moments of complicity, laughter, joint projects and precious memories can enrich the lives of spouses and strengthen their emotional bond.

Ultimately, a successful marriage is much more than just a personal achievement.

It's the fruit of a mutual commitment, an ongoing investment in the relationship, and a willingness to cultivate love, understanding and respect within the couple. It's a precious achievement that can bring deep satisfaction, lasting happiness and a sense of fulfillment to each partner's life.

Chapter 19. Examples of remarkably successful personalities

Numerous personalities around the world have embodied the concept of success in various fields, often overcoming considerable obstacles to achieve their goals. Their journeys can serve as inspiration and role models for those seeking success in their own lives. Here are a few emblematic examples:

1. ** Barack Obama **

Barack Obama is a remarkable example of success and perseverance, a story that continues to inspire millions of people around the world. His 2008 presidential campaign, under the slogan "Yes We Can", became a symbol of hope and change, not just in the United States but worldwide. This slogan captured the essence of a movement that believed deeply in the possibility of renewal and transformation at a time of economic and social challenge.

Obama's legacy therefore extends beyond America's borders, inspiring leaders and individuals to create positive change in their communities and beyond. The trajectory of his life is a reminder that, despite the obstacles, with determination and a collective spirit, "Yes We Can" can become a reality for everyone.

2. **Steve Jobs** - Co-founder of Apple Inc, Jobs is famous for revolutionizing many industries, from personal computing and animation to music and mobile telephony. His journey, marked by highs and lows, symbolizes perseverance and innovation.

3. **Oprah Winfrey** - From very modest living conditions and

Oprah has become one of the world's most influential media personalities. Host, producer and philanthropist, she has used her platform to promote education, health and well-being.

4. **Nelson Mandela** - An emblematic figure in South Africa's fight against apartheid, Mandela spent 27 years in prison before becoming the country's first black president. His dedication to the cause of freedom and equality won him worldwide recognition and the Nobel Peace Prize.

5. ** Youssou N'Dour - Youssou N'Dour's career embodies a multi-dimensional success story. It shows that beyond personal and professional success, the ability to positively influence society and fight for important causes is an essential facet of success. As an artist, entrepreneur and politician, Youssou N'Dour continues to inspire people around the world with his talent, vision and unwavering commitment to the well-being and advancement of his community and continent.

Beyond his impressive career as a Senegalese musician, singer and songwriter, Youssou N'Dour has also played a significant role as a philanthropist and entrepreneur, helping to create jobs and support young people in his country and beyond.

6. **Marie Curie** - A Polish-born physicist and chemist, Marie Curie was the first woman to win a Nobel Prize, and remains to this day the only person to have won two in two different sciences (physics and chemistry). Her discoveries in radioactivity paved the way for significant advances in science and medicine.

7. **Aliko Dangote is a leading example of business success in Africa and internationally. From very little, Dangote has built an industrial and commercial empire that focuses on the production of cement, sugar, flour, salt and, more recently, oil refining and agriculture.

Aliko Dangote's example is a source of inspiration for many entrepreneurs in Africa and around the world. His success underlines the importance of vision, perseverance, adaptability and social commitment in the entrepreneurial journey.

8. **Elon Musk** - A successful entrepreneur in fields as diverse as online payments (PayPal), electric cars (Tesla), and space exploration (SpaceX), Musk is often cited as an embodiment of innovation and ambition in the modern tech business world.

9. **Malala Yousafzai** - A Pakistani campaigner for girls' education and the youngest winner of the Nobel Peace Prize, Malala became a global symbol of courage and resistance in the face of oppression after surviving an assassination attempt by the Taliban.

10. **Serena Williams** - Considered one of the greatest female athletes of all time, Serena Williams dominated women's tennis for more than two decades, winning 23 Grand Slam singles titles and many more in doubles, all the while overcoming injuries and personal obstacles.

These individuals illustrate that success can take many forms - whether entrepreneurial, scientific, sporting, or contributions to society. Although their fields of activity are varied, they all share a deep commitment to pursuing their passions and overcoming challenges, showing that the road to success is often paved with perseverance, determination, and an unshakeable will to make a difference in the world.

Conclusion

Success, whether defined in personal, professional, relational or other terms, can be a deeply enriching and meaningful pursuit in anyone's life. It goes beyond the simple achievement of goals or the attainment of certain conventional standards of success.

Success can also teach the importance of adaptability and resilience. Facing challenges, bouncing back from adversity, adapting to change and the unexpected are key skills for navigating the path to success.

Ultimately, success is a personal and subjective quest, involving challenges, triumphs, lessons and moments of joy. It can take many and varied forms, but is often associated with the pursuit of one's aspirations, the development of harmonious relationships, and a sense of personal fulfillment. Whether in the professional, family, relationship or personal sphere, success can be a path to satisfaction, happiness and fulfillment in life.

ACKNOWLEDGEMENTS

Dear readers,

In this moment of reflection and gratitude, I would like to express my sincere thanks to those who have shaped the man I am today. To my parents for the caring upbringing and profound values they instilled in me, I am eternally grateful. Every life lesson, every moment of love and support has formed the foundation of my journey.

Dedication

To my dear mother, who now rests in peace and whose sweet memory continues to light my way, may the land of Yoff be light to her. Your sacrifices, wisdom and unconditional love remain a constant inspiration in my life. You will always be present in my heart and thoughts, guiding me with kindness from where you watch over us.

To my father, a father figure who inspired and guided me throughout my apprenticeship, my reference.

To my sister, Mané, you've been my partner in crime, my confidante and my example of generosity and strength. Thank you for sharing life's ups and downs with me, for showing me the value of mutual help and unconditional love. To my brothers and sisters, who have always been there for me, I send you all my gratitude and love.

To my wife Nina, to Annie and to Saïd,

for their boundless kindness, their unfailing support and the delicious meals that have brightened up our family moments, I thank you from the bottom of my heart. Your presence in my life is a precious gift that I cherish every day.

Finally, to my teachers, I owe you a huge debt of gratitude. Your knowledge, encouragement and commitment have nourished my thirst for knowledge and helped me grow as an individual.

To all those who have crossed my path and contributed to my personal and professional growth, I offer my sincerest thanks. Your teachings, love and support have been the cornerstones of my success and development.

Thank you for everything.

With gratitude,

Madiop Auguste DIALLO

Glossary :

Dollar-cost averaging = spreading the dollar hit

ETFs = Exchange Traded Funds

SEO = Search Engine Optimization

Freelancers = freelancers

SCPI (Sociétés Civiles de Placement Immobilier)

REITs: Real Estate Investment Trusts

Crowdfunding: is the exchange of funds between individuals outside the institutional financial circuits, in order to finance a project via an online platform.

Biography

Name: Madiop Auguste DIALLO

Madiop Auguste DIALLO is a French-Senegalese software engineer with a passion for technology and literature. He graduated from SUPINFO INTERNATIONAL UNIVERSITY DE PARIS with a specialization in software engineering.

Passionate about the versatility of languages, Auguste is trilingual, mastering French, English and his native Wolof. He uses this skill in his work to build bridges between different international teams,

In addition to his technical expertise, Auguste spends his free time learning new languages and exploring comparative linguistics. This passion enables him to immerse himself in diverse cultures and integrate these experiences into his approaches to solving IT problems.

Today, Auguste continues to invest in the development of solutions that broaden the horizons of the e-book, while preparing a collection of short stories inspired by the stories behind the algorithms he encounters on a daily basis. His life is a rich tapestry where the threads of prose and computer code intertwine, both woven with equal and boundless passion.

TABLE OF CONTENTS

Chapter 1. The Definition of Success

Chapter 2. Self-knowledge

Chapter 3: Setting achievable goals

Chapter 4. Perseverance

Chapter 5: Surround yourself with the good guys

Chapter 6. Time Management

Chapter 7. Getting to know banks

Chapter 8. Personal finance

Chapter 9. Continuous learning

Chapter 10. The important thing is not how much you earn but how you earn it

Chapter 11. The desire to succeed.

Chapter 12. The keys to success

Chapter 13. Daring to take on challenges

Chapter 14. Generating income with small amounts of capital

Chapter 15. Learning to invest

Chapter 16. Cryptocurrencies, dividends, gold

Chapter 17. Real estate companies and subleases

Chapter 18. Success makes you happy

Chapter 19. Examples of remarkably successful personalities.

Conclusion

Thanks

Lexicon

Biography

www.ingramcontent.com/pod-product-compliance
Lightning Source LLC
Chambersburg PA
CBHW052200220526

45471CB00004B/1755